Forensic Science

Ron Fridell

LERNER BOOKS • LONDON • NEW YORK • MINNEAPOLIS

First published in the United Kingdom in 2008 by
Lerner Books,
Dalton House,
60 Windsor Avenue,
London SW19 2RR

Website address: www.lernerbooks.co.uk

This edition was updated and edited for UK publication by Discovery Books Ltd.,
Unit 3, 37 Watling Street, Leintwardine, Shropshire SY7 0LW

British Library Cataloguing in Publication Data

Fridell, Ron
Forensic science. - (Cool science)
1. Criminal investigation - Juvenile literature 2. Crime scene searches - Juvenile literature 3. Forensic sciences - Juvenile literature
I. Title
363.2'5

ISBN-13: 978 1 58013 422 4

Printed in China

Table of Contents

Introduction

Picture a burglar fleeing the scene of the crime in the dead of night. He just broke into a house and ran off with cash and jewellery. A high fence surrounds the house. A police officer is in hot pursuit. The thief dashes for the fence.

A row of iron spikes runs along the top of the fence. The burglar grabs onto a spike with each hand. He pulls himself up and hauls himself over. As he leaps down, a scream fills the night air.

You can leave clues about your identity in many different places. A criminal climbing over a fence may leave evidence of himself behind.

The burglar runs off into the darkness. A police officer shines a light along the top of the fence. Something dark catches his eye. He climbs up for a closer look. Blood coats one of the spikes on the fence. The thief must have cut himself as he climbed over the fence.

'Ouch!' the officer says to himself.

Later, the burglar is arrested. He left the police a clue that tells them exactly who he is. Can you work out the clue?

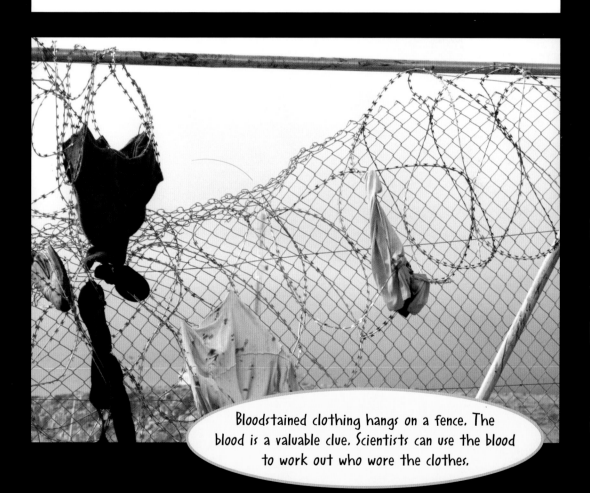

Bloodstained clothing hangs on a fence. The blood is a valuable clue. Scientists can use the blood to work out who wore the clothes.

Answer: The burglar left behind a sample of his genetic code, his DNA. This blood matches a DNA profile of a suspect on the police's database. Turn to page 25 to find out more about DNA.

chapter 1

Hard Evidence

A fingerprint on a freshly painted railing helped catch a criminal. So did a layer of dust on a roof beam and skin cells stuck to a stocking. Crime solvers used forensic science to make sense of these clues.

The word *forensic* means 'used in courts of law'. Forensic science helps police to solve crimes. It is a way of finding and analysing clues.

Forensic scientists may find fingerprints on a dusty beam help to solve a crime.

The clues can be used as evidence in court. Evidence is anything used to prove that a certain person is guilty or not guilty of committing a crime. Here's how forensic science led police to a terrorist.

Tracking Down a Terrorist

On 19 April, 1995 an explosion shook Oklahoma City in the United States of America. Objects went flying everywhere. A piece of metal flew 175 metres and crashed into the windshield of a car. The piece of metal came from the axle of a van. The van had carried a 2,300-kilogram bomb. The bomb blast tore off the entire front of the Alfred P Murrah Federal Building. It killed 168 people inside.

A search team found the metal from the van's axle. The axle had part of the vehicle identification number (VIN) on it. Every car, lorry and van carries a unique VIN.

The VIN led federal agents, or investigators, to a van rental shop in Junction City, Kansas. The person who worked there remembered the man who had rented the van. The man had used the name Robert Kling. The name was fake, but the shop assistant remembered his face.

IT'S A FACT!

The 1995 Oklahoma City bombing killed 168 people, injured more than eight hundred people, and destroyed or seriously damaged more than three hundred buildings.

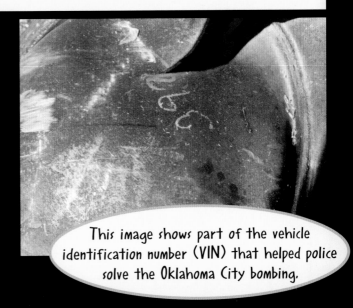

This image shows part of the vehicle identification number (VIN) that helped police solve the Oklahoma City bombing.

Police used an artist's sketch (left) to identify Timothy McVeigh (below).

A forensic artist made a sketch from the clerk's description. The owner of a hotel recognized the face. It looked like a man who had stayed there. His name was Timothy McVeigh.

Agents ran McVeigh's name through a national crime computer database. He was in jail in Perry, Oklahoma, USA. Police were holding McVeigh on a minor offence. They were about to set him free.

Agents caught up with him just in time. Timothy McVeigh was tried, convicted and executed, all because of a piece of metal.

McVeigh's Motive

Timothy McVeigh was a terrorist. Terrorists use violence to scare people into doing what they want. Often terrorists want to change a government. McVeigh attacked a US federal building – a building used by the government – to show that he did not like the US government. He thought the bombing would persuade other people to join him in a war against the government.

Two Types of Evidence

Courts rely on two types of evidence. One is information from eyewitnesses. These are people who saw something related to the crime – the shop assistant for example. However, eyewitness information can't always be trusted. Witnesses may get confused, forget details or change their minds. They may even lie to protect themselves or their friends.

The second type of evidence is forensic evidence. An example is the VIN number on McVeigh's axle. Forensic evidence never gets confused. It never forgets and it never lies. It's sometimes called hard evidence. Forensic evidence helps catch and convict thousands of criminals each year. It wasn't always like this, though.

Criminals Catching Criminals

In 1810, the city of Paris, France, hired François-Eugène Vidocq (right) to head its undercover police force. It was a risky choice. Vidocq had been a tough criminal. However, Vidocq knew exactly how other criminals worked. For many years, he worked to help keep the streets of Paris safe.

ITS A FACT!

In 1817, Vidocq and his twelve assistants made more than eight hundred arrests.

A little more than one hundred years ago, scientists were just starting to study crime. In Italy in the 1870s, Dr Cesare Lombroso looked at the faces and bodies of about six thousand criminals. He thought that certain types of criminals looked alike. He said that people who started fires had small heads. Robbers had thick hair and pickpockets had long hands!

The doctor was wrong. You can't tell if people are good or bad based on how they look. Lombroso's efforts were still important, though. They hinted that forensic science was about to be born.

Dr Cesare Lombroso.

In 1887, author Arthur Conan Doyle began publishing the Sherlock Holmes stories. Holmes was a fictional detective. In the stories, he lived in an apartment at 221b Baker Street in London. It was like a crime lab (laboratory). Holmes had reference books, a magnifying glass and chemicals for finding clues. Holmes used forensic science to discover things the police had missed. Readers loved the stories. They wished this detective was real.

A British magazine published this drawing of Sherlock Holmes (right) and his friend Dr Watson (left) in the late 1800s.

Fact finally caught up with fiction in 1910, when the world's first crime lab opened. The lab was in Lyon, France. The real-life Sherlock Holmes was French police detective Edmond Locard.

Historians call Locard the father of forensic science. He gave the police powerful new tools. Locard showed how microscopes could be used to help solve crimes. Another tool was an idea about how to find clues. 'When two objects come into contact with each other, they exchange trace evidence', he wrote. This idea is called Locard's Exchange Principle. Trace evidence may be very small, such as a few fibres from a suspect's shirt that are underneath a victim's fingernails. In the next case, Locard used his big idea and a microscope to catch three criminals.

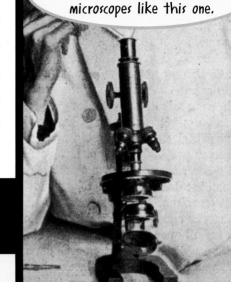

The world's first crime labs used microscopes like this one.

Catching Criminals with a Microscope

Soon after Locard set up his crime lab, the police went to him with a difficult case. Some people were making fake coins and spending them in Lyon. Someone who makes fake money is called a counterfeiter. The police had an idea who the counterfeiters were, but they couldn't find the evidence to arrest them.

Locard asked for some of the suspects' clothing. Using some tweezers, he removed every last speck of dust from the inside of the suspects' trouser pockets. Then he brushed the dust from their shirtsleeves onto sheets of white paper.

Each particle then went under the microscope. Locard had already analysed the fake coins. They were made of three metals. He found those same three metals in the men's clothing: tin, antimony and lead. The criminals were caught and convicted.

Edmond Locard used science to solve hundreds more crimes. Modern crime solvers still rely on his exchange principle. As we look at more cases, we will see them use it again and again.

chapter 2

Investigating Crime Scenes

The work of solving a crime often begins with a 999 emergency call. The operator taking the 999 calls tells police units where to go. The police speed to the scene.

Crime scenes come in many shapes and sizes. Police may find a car with a murder victim inside. They might arrive at a house that's been looted by burglars. They may find heaps of rubble where a building once stood such as at the scene of the Oklahoma City bombing.

An operator takes a call at a 999 call centre in Surrey. A 999 call is often the first step in solving crime.

Taking Care

The first thing police must do is to secure the crime scene. They surround small spaces with blue and white tape. To seal off larger spaces, they call in extra police officers. Those officers guard the scene and help to look for evidence.

The officers make sure not to touch anything or walk on anything that might be a clue. They do not use the telephone. Only certain people enter the crime scene. Some of these people will be Scenes of Crime Officers or SOCOs. In the United States of America SOCOs are known as Crime Scene Investigators or CSIs.

Yellow tape marks a crime scene (*top*). Investigators carefully search for evidence (*bottom*) at the burial site of a murder victim.

SOCOs are police officers who search crime scenes for forensic evidence. They collect any weapons that are on the scene. If someone was shot, the SOCOs look for bullets. Bullets can be matched to the guns that fired them. The science of matching bullets to guns is ballistics.

Most forensic evidence is much harder to find than a weapon. A SOCO must be a skilful observer. SOCOs always watch for details that don't seem to fit, as in the following case.

Caught by a Dusty Detail

The year is 1925, somewhere in the United Kingdom. A man is trying to get away with murder. He tells police he found his wife dead. He says she was hanging by a rope she had tied to a roof beam. He claims that he cut her down and removed the rope before calling police.

Then investigators go to work on the crime scene. Everything seems to fit. At ground level, it looks like the husband is telling the truth. Then the police look up at the ceiling.

There's a clue on the roof beam where the man says the rope was tied. The dusty beam has not been touched or disturbed. No rope was tied here. The husband is lying.

Police and SOCOs can find clues almost anywhere. A dusty beam, the angle at which a noose hangs, fibre samples or footprints in the mud may all yield valuable evidence.

Powerful Prints

Everyone's fingerprints are unique. That makes fingerprints powerful evidence. Fingerprints at the scene of a crime prove that the person who made the prints has been there.

SOCOs know the most likely places to find prints. In cars, they look at such things as door handles and seat belt buckles. In houses, they look at door-knobs, phones, light switches and windows.

Fingerprints can also show up in sur-prising places. In one case, the crimi-nals wiped down an entire apartment. They tried to get rid of every last one of their fingerprints. They forgot one thing. The criminals' prints were on dirty plates, glasses, and silver-ware inside the dishwasher.

No two people have the same fingerprint.

Your fingerprints are unique. You can be identified from them.

Collecting Trace

Collecting trace evidence – also known as trace – is slow. It calls for skill and patience. SOCOs use special tools to remove tiny things from all sorts of surfaces. Clear, sticky tape lifts bits of evidence from rugs and tables. A vacuum cleaner with special filters collects trace from the in-sides of cars. Nail files scrape trace from under fingernails.

SOCOs collect trace with one unbreakable rule in mind: never overlook anything. Even a single matchstick near a victim's body could lead to a matchbox in a suspect's pocket.

Traces of You
Look carefully in your own pockets. What could a SOCO or forensic investigator tell about you from the evidence there?

Fishing for Evidence

Each SOCO carries a crime kit (*below*) for gathering evidence at the scene. A kit contains many different items. Here are a few:

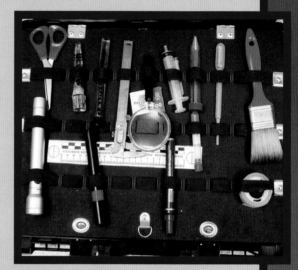

- tape to secure crime scene
- a digital camera
- a torch
- containers, such as paper and plastic bags, for storing evidence
- fingerprinting tools, including powder, brush and clear tape
- a vacuum with special filters for collecting trace evidence

SOCOs may buy ready-made crime kits or put together their own. Some use fishing tackle boxes to carry their equipment.

How much can SOCOs learn from trace evidence collected at a crime scene? Let's find out.

The Amazing Trace Case

It is 1923 in a remote part of southern Oregon, USA. A gang tries to rob a train. They murder the train crew and then run away. When police arrive, they find nothing but a pair of greasy overalls – not much to go on.

The police send the overalls to Edward Heinrich. He is head of the forensics lab in Berkeley, California, USA. Can he find clues to lead them to the criminals?

Heinrich examines the overalls and makes his report. Police are amazed at the results. Heinrich directs them to look for a left-handed forester who is 1.8 metres tall, weighs about 75 kg, has light brown hair, is in his early twenties, rolls his own cigarettes and is careful about his personal appearance.

ITS A FACT!

Forensic scientist Edward Heinrich solved more than two thousand cases in his career.

How could all these clues come from a single piece of clothing? Heinrich explains. Left-handed? The pockets on the left-hand side are more worn out than those on the right. The owner's height and weight? The size of the overalls shows that. The hair colour came from a hair stuck to a button. Heinrich also used the hair to work out the owner's age. Bits of tobacco in the pockets mean he must roll his own cigarettes. Nail clippings in a seam suggest he has a neat appearance.

How does he know the suspect is a forester? Those greasy marks on the overalls are sap. The sap is from trees that foresters cut down in the forests of southern Oregon.

One final piece of incriminating evidence – a scrap of paper was stuck in a pocket of his overalls. It must have been there for months. It was faded from many washes. However, when Heinrich treated it with iodine, the words written on it came back. It was a postal receipt for a package sent to Roy D'Autremont.

Not all trees are alike. Sap from a tree may tell police where a suspect has been.

The police go to D'Autremont's address. They talk to his neighbours. Heinrich's description fits the man perfectly. Roy and brothers Ray and Hugh have been missing since the day of the robbery.

It took police four years, but they finally tracked down all three brothers. The men confessed to the crime and were sent to prison.

The D'Autremont brothers (from left to right), Hugh, Roy and Ray had been living under different names when police tracked them down.

The Chain of Custody

Besides being good observers, forensic investigators must be careful people. They have to follow rules to maintain the chain of custody. Custody means taking care of something. Forensic investigators keep track of each piece of evidence. The first link in the chain is the moment a clue is discovered. The final link is the day the evidence is used in court.

Let's say the clue is a drop of blood. The blood is found on a wooden floor at the scene of a murder. The blood must be collected from the wooden surface. Then it is sealed in a container that is properly labelled and taken to a police station. There, the blood is logged in as evidence and sent to a lab for analysis.

Each of these steps is a link in the chain of custody. Each link must be made properly. Any mistakes could weaken even the strongest forensic evidence in a court of law, as the next case shows.

Freed by Forensic Mistakes

Crime Scene Investigators had enough forensic evidence to prove that O J Simpson was a murderer. On 12 June, 1994 Simpson's ex-wife, Nicole Brown Simpson and her friend, Ron Goldman were murdered. Simpson, a retired American football star, said he had nothing to do with the crime, but police suspected otherwise.

The evidence included traces of the victims' blood found on Simpson's socks and in his car. Police also found Simpson's blood at the crime scene.

CSIs, police officers and lab workers from the Los Angeles Police Department (LAPD) made mistakes. They did not handle the evidence according to the rules. One officer was supposed to take bloody evidence straight to the police station. Instead, he left it in his hot van for a few hours. Heat can damage evidence.

A detective points to the glove found on Nicole Simpson's bloody path (top). A detective holds the shovel found in O J's van the morning of the murders.

Simpson's lawyers did not question the forensic evidence. Instead, they questioned what the LAPD did with it. The lawyers said that poor investigating violated the chain of custody.

Simpson's lawyers made the jury doubt the work of the LAPD. As a result, the jury found O J Simpson not guilty. The moral of the story? Even the best forensic evidence may not be enough. The people in the chain of custody have to handle it according to the rules.

chapter 3

Who Are You?

How do your fingerprints get from your skin to surfaces such as doorknobs and tabletops? Give the tips of your fingers a close look. Use a magnifying glass. You'll see elevated ridges with cracks running between. The lines run in curves and circles and loops.

Just beneath the skin are sweat glands. The glands ooze oils through tiny holes called pores. Sweat or perspiration, is nearly all water, but not quite. About 1.5 per cent is a mix of salt and chemicals. This mix remains on your fingertips after the water evaporates. This salty residue is transferred to a surface when you touch it. In this way, you leave behind a print.

Your fingerprints begin forming before your birth. By the time you're born, they are complete and permanent. They will always provide positive proof of who you are.

ITS A FACT!
If you cut or burn your finger, the skin will grow back with the same fingerprint you had before.

Caught by Wet Paint

Tens of thousands of criminals have been caught by their fingerprints. One of the earliest cases was in 1902, in the United Kingdom.

A robbery had taken place in Dulwich, south-east London. A detective had managed to retrieve a fingerprint from a freshly painted board near the crime scene. The fingerprint appeared to match that of a well-known burglar called Henry Jackson. He was arrested and taken to Brixton prison in south London. Here he was fingerprinted again for a positive match.

This was an interesting case because the prosecuting barrister was able to explain fingerprinting techniques to the jury – and gain a conviction. Henry Jackson received a sentence of seven years in prison.

Collect and Compare

To every SOCO, the words *dusting* and *lifting* have a special meaning. They describe what SOCOs must do to collect fingerprints at a crime scene. First, they dust the surface with a special powder. They apply it with a camel hair brush, using short, quick strokes. The dust sticks to the salty residue on a fingerprint. Then SOCOs press clear tape down onto the surface and carefully lift it back up. The tape now contains the fingerprint. The tape is then put on a piece of paper or card. SOCO's also make sure the evidence is labelled correctly.

An SOCO dusts a glass for fingerprints (top). She carefully labels the evidence (right).

Later, forensics experts can compare crime scene fingerprints with the prints they have on file. In the United Kingdom, for example, police forces use a computer database, called IDENT1. The fingerprints, and sometimes the palm prints, of criminal suspects are taken when they are arrested. Special scanners are sometimes used to digitally record the prints. This information is then stored in the computer database. IDENT1 has millions of prints on file. Unknown prints from a crime scene can be compared with the millions on file to get a match. This job takes just a few minutes. Before the computer age, this would have taken much, much longer. IDENT1 is used to identify prints at around 78,000 crime scenes each year.

IT'S A FACT!
The FBI has fingerprint records for around 47 million people in the US.

A suspect's fingerprints are scanned. They will be stored in the IDENT1 database.

Caught by Superglue

Richard Ramirez was known as the Night Stalker. Ramirez was a serial killer. He killed many people and he chose his victims at random. He killed most of his victims at night. In California, during 1984 and 1985, Ramirez killed at least thirteen people, but then he made a mistake.

In August 1985, Ramirez attacked two people. Both people survived. One of the victims saw him drive off in a Toyota. A neighbour also saw the Toyota. The neighbour gave police the registration number.

They tracked the car down in Los Angeles, where Ramirez had abandoned it.

Forensic investigators used a special technique to search the car for fingerprints. They put a plate of special superglue inside and closed the doors and windows. Soon the superglue fumes spread throughout the inside of the car. Wherever there were fingerprints, the fumes would react with the skin oil.

Later, investigators used a laser – a narrow, powerful beam of light – to search the interior. They found a single fingerprint. When they

The Night Stalker, Richard Ramirez, killed at least thirteen people in thirteen months in the mid-1980s.

ran the print through their database, they came up with a match. Ramirez had been arrested years earlier for a minor crime. His fingerprints were on file.

So the police knew *who* the Night Stalker was, but they didn't know *where* he was. They sent his photograph to newspapers and TV stations all over California.

On 31 August, 1985 Ramirez tried to steal another car. The owner fought him off. People on the street recognized Ramirez from his photograph, and they chased and caught him. In November 1989, Richard Ramirez was sentenced to death. He remains on Death Row.

DNA Profiling

In 1984, Dr Alec Jeffreys at Leicester University found a new way to identify people. The key was deoxyribonucleic acid or DNA. Nearly all the cells in your body contain DNA. This amazing molecule tells your body how to keep you alive and make you grow.

DNA is made of a spiral-shaped ladder of chemicals. This ladder is known as the human genome. Most of this microscopic ladder is the same in all people. Your genome is about 98 per cent the same as everyone else's. Certain strands of this chemical ladder are as unique to you as your fingerprints.

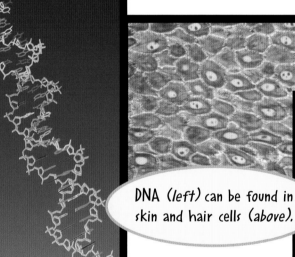

DNA *(left)* can be found in skin and hair cells *(above)*.

Scientists have discovered how to look at these unique strands of DNA. The result is called a DNA profile. Scientists can get a profile from sweat, saliva, blood and even skin cells left at the scene of a crime.

A scientist studies a DNA profile.

Like fingerprints, DNA profiles can be stored on computer databases and searched for matches. Like fingerprints, courts accept DNA profiles as evidence. DNA profiles are especially useful in a cold case. That's a crime that has gone unsolved for many years, like the one on the next page.

DNA and a Cold Case

In 1986, Nick Calabrese gunned down John Fecarotta. Both men were members of Chicago mobs. Mobs are organized gangs of professional criminals, who often use violence to get what they want.

It was not a clean killing. There was a struggle. Calabrese was shot too, but he survived. The gloves he wore got soaked in his own blood. Calabrese left before police arrived, but police found one of the gloves in a litter bin near the crime scene. They stored the glove as evidence.

The case remained unsolved until 2002. That year, an informant (a person who secretly helps police) told police that Calabrese had killed Fecarotta. So police got a DNA sample from Calabrese. This is as simple as touching the inside of the suspect's mouth with a cotton swab. The traces of saliva are enough to give the suspect's DNA profile.

A scientist uses a cotton swab to take a DNA sample.

In 1986, police could not get a DNA profile from the bloody glove. However in 2002, they could. The profile of the blood on the glove matched the profile from Calabrese's saliva. That proved he was at the crime scene.

When police showed Calabrese the matching profiles, he knew he was doomed. So Calabrese confessed to Fecarotta's murder. He agreed to give police information about mob activities. In exchange, he was sentenced to prison but did not get the death penalty.

Fingerprints and DNA evidence can positively answer the question, *Who are you?* They can place a suspect at the scene of a crime and help convict the suspect. However, fingerprints and DNA evidence are not foolproof. Mistakes can lead police in the wrong direction, as in these cases.

Lips, Ears, Teeth

In some cases, suspects have been identified by lip prints and even ear prints they left at the crime scene. Bite marks can also lead police to a suspect.

Wrong Prints, Wrong Profile

On 11 March, 2004 terrorists blew up subway trains in Madrid, Spain. Nearly two hundred people died. The FBI joined police in Spain to help track down the terrorists. The evidence they found included bomb materials sealed in a plastic bag. A fingerprint was on the bag.

FBI experts compared the print on the bag with prints in databases. They came up with a match. FBI agents said matching prints belonged to a lawyer from Portland, USA.

A few weeks later, fingerprint experts in Spain said the print belonged to another man. He was from the North African country of Algeria. The FBI agreed. They had been wrong about the lawyer.

Even DNA profiling is not completely foolproof. In 2004, DNA profiling linked a woman to a burglary. Authorities said that DNA found at the scene positively matched her profile. Later, they discovered the woman could not possibly have been the burglar. She was in prison when the burglary took place, serving time for another crime.

Was there something wrong with the forensic evidence? No. In both cases it was the experts who were wrong. They did not look at all the evidence closely enough. They jumped to wrong conclusions.

Skulls, Bones, Teeth

Suppose you had only a person's bones to look at. How much could you work out about that person?

Forensic anthropologists study skeletal remains. Sometimes a skeleton tells how a person died. A bullet hole or a knife cut can show up on the skull or bones. Bones may hold chemical traces of poisoning too, even years after death.

Bones can also reveal things about who the victims were. For one thing, they can reveal the sex. Male bones tend to be broader at the ends. In addition, the bony ridge along the brow is usually larger. A female's pelvis is generally broader than a male's. Scientists can also tell the person's approximate age and height.

Bones — whether a complete skeleton or just a skull — can hold a lot of valuable information for forensic scientists.

You and Your Bones

Your body has 206 bones. The average adult female's bones weigh about 14.5 kg. The average male's bones weigh about 15.4 kg. The rest of the body's weight is tissue — including muscles and organs — hair and fluids.

Bones give hints about the person's race too. Investigators put all these clues together to learn more about the victim.

Sometimes forensic anthropologists can even work out the person's occupation. A flute player's teeth and mouth bones take on a distinctive look after years of playing. A manual labourer's spine may be bent from carrying heavy loads. A carpenter's teeth are often chipped from holding nails between them.

Forensic dentists are able to identify the dead by their teeth. What makes one person's teeth different from another's? Width, thickness and spacing of teeth vary for each person. Chipping and grinding also make teeth unique. Then there are the distinctive signs of dental work, as in the case that follows.

Paul Revere's Teeth

Paul Revere was best known for his midnight ride during the American Revolution (1775–1783). He rode from Boston to Lexington, Massachusetts. He warned American colonists that the British soldiers were coming.

Revere also worked as a dentist. He made an unusual set of false teeth for his friend, Dr Joseph Warren. They were held together with silver wire. Revere used part of a hippopotamus tusk for the teeth.

In June 1775, Dr Warren was killed at the Battle of Bunker Hill. His body was buried

Paul Revere (right) was a metalworker, a dentist and an American patriot.

in a grave with other soldiers. Warren's family wanted to give the body a proper burial. Revere had the grave dug up and the bodies brought out. He was able to identify Warren's body from the distinctive teeth he had made for his close friend.

Reconstructing Faces

Picture a skull. Imagine putting the skin, hair, ears, eyes, nose, teeth, lips, cheeks and chin back on it. This is what forensic sculptors do. Their job is to recreate the missing faces of unknown victims long after death.

This process is called facial reconstruction. It begins with the skull itself or a plaster cast of it. The artist drills small holes and inserts pegs of different heights. The pegs help the artist know how thick the skin should be in different parts of the face. Then clay is added to fill in the spaces between the pegs. It begins to look like skin rising and falling over muscles and bones. The artist then forms the nose, lips and other features. A wig and artificial eyes are added. Make-up helps make the clay look more like skin.

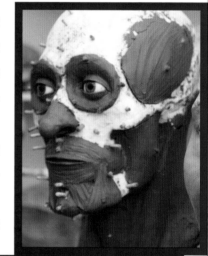

The final product is not meant to look exactly like the victim's face. However, if it is done well, it will be similar to the person's actual face. Sometimes facial reconstruction helps bring a guilty person to justice, as in the following case.

Forensic artists can use a skull to create a model of someone's face.

A Face from the Grave

In Missouri, USA in 1988, a woman's skeleton was found in a shallow grave. No one knew who she was. So police used a forensic artist to reconstruct the face from the skull.

A woman in Missouri saw photographs of the reconstructed face. She called the police. The face looked like her neighbour. The neighbour had been missing since 1983. The missing woman's name was Bun Chee Nyhuis. Police talked to her husband. He said she left him five years ago.

Police took a photograph of Bun Chee Nyhuis to Michael Charney. He is a forensic anthropologist. They also sent him a photo of the skull. Did the skull and the face in the photo belong to the same person?

Skulls can be compared with old photographs to help work out who the person was.

Charney used video skull-face superimposition to find out. Superimposition means putting one thing on top of another. First, he marked the face area in each photo at the same thirty points. Then he had the two marked photographs put onto videotape.

Using two video cameras, he projected the photos of the woman and the skull side by side onto a screen. Then, slowly, he moved one image on top of the other. All thirty points on the two images locked tightly together. The face fitted the skull perfectly. Confronted with this forensic evidence, the husband confessed to murdering his wife.

chapter 4

What Happened?

To solve a case, investigators must reconstruct the crime. For violent crimes, they need to know the time and cause of death. Work begins straight away. The forensic scientist is always one of the first investigators on the scene.

The forensic scientist will officially determine time and cause of death. Whereas the SOCOs investigate the crime scene, the forensic scientist investigates the body.

To find the time of death, the forensic scientist takes the body's internal temperature. Body temperature starts falling the moment the victim dies. A normal living person is about 37°C. For the first twelve hours after death, the temperature falls at the rate of about 0.6°C per hour. After that, it falls about half as fast. Certain things may change how fast the temperature falls. These include the victim's size, the amount of clothing the victim wore and the surrounding temperature.

To find cause of death, the forensic scientist examines the outside of the body. Are there any wounds? If so, what sort of weapon might have made them? When the forensic scientist is finished, the body is wrapped in a sheet, zipped into a body bag and taken to the morgue, (where dead bodies are kept before they are buried).

Fingerprinting the Dead

Later, the forensic scientist may do a post-mortem, if possible. They use a special stainless steel table with a drain. It funnels body fluids into a tank on the floor. Scales are used to weigh each internal organ. A smaller table nearby is for cutting up and examining the organs.

GALWAY COUNTY LIBRARIES

Before the post-mortem, the body is weighed and measured. Then it's photographed and X-rayed. Any identifying marks are noted. These include tattoos, scars and injuries. The forensic scientist collects any trace evidence on the body, such as loose hairs. The forensic scientist may clean and clip fingernails. Then it's time for fingerprinting.

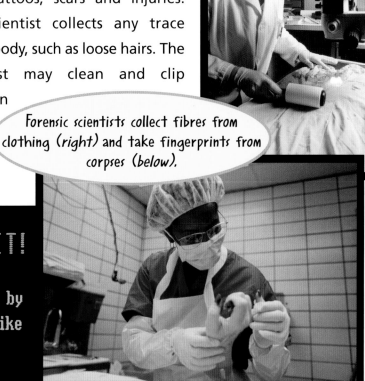

Forensic scientists collect fibres from clothing (right) and take fingerprints from corpses (below).

IT'S A FACT!

The body of a person poisoned by cyanide smells like bitter almonds.

Fingerprints can be taken with ink and paper, in most cases. However, if the body has been dead for a long time, the fingertips may be too shrivelled and dry. Then the forensic scientist must amputate them and soak each one in water until the skin softens. The forensic scientist places each amputated finger in a separate, numbered bottle.

Sometimes the fingertip skin is so loose that it falls off the bone. The forensic scientist may then pull on a glove and place each of the corpse's fingertips over his or her own fingers. Then the forensic scientist rolls each one in ink and presses it onto paper to make the print.

The Post-Mortem

The forensic scientist looks closely at the eyes and eyelids of the corpse. If the victim has been strangled, pinprick-size spots called petechiae will show up on the skin near the eyes. This is where bleeding has occurred.

Then the hard work begins. The forensic scientist opens up the chest and removes the internal organs – such as the heart and lungs. Each organ is weighed and examined for damage. The stomach is removed, and the contents are stored for lab examination later on.

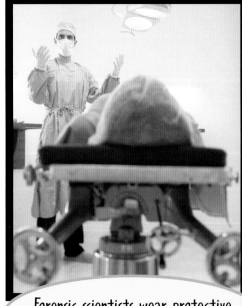

Then it's time for the head. The forensic scientist cuts through the scalp from ear to ear and folds over a flap. The skull can then be sawed open and the brain removed. It too is examined and weighed. The forensic scientist takes cell samples

Forensic scientists wear protective clothing during a post-mortem.

from the brain and other organs and bodily fluids. These samples will be sent to another lab for testing.

After the post-mortem examination is done, the internal organs are returned to the body. The chest and head are sewn up. A normal post-mortem takes about two hours. During the post-mortem, the forensic scientist describes it using a voice recorder.

The Yuck Factor

How can forensic scientists do their job without feeling sick or passing out? Maybe they're a little different from the rest of us. Michael Baden, says he was never disgusted by seeing a corpse dissected. When he was still a student, he saw a victim who had died of gunshot wounds. 'It was a good learning experience', he said.

Time of Death

Internal body temperature is only one way that forensic scientists work out the time of death. A second is *livor mortis.* That's what happens to a person's blood after death. It changes colour as the force of gravity pushes it slowly downwards. The parts of the body facing upwards get pale. The parts facing down turn purple.

Rigor mortis is another time-of-death factor. These Latin words mean 'the stiffness of death'. The muscles start stiffening shortly after death. First, it's the small muscles in the face. Then the rigor mortis spreads downwards into the neck and beyond, all the way to the toes. If a body is completely stiff, the person has probably been dead for about twelve hours. Once rigor mortis has set in, the process reverses. After about forty-eight hours, the whole body is relaxed again.

The forensic scientist must also consider the climate. A cold climate preserves a body. Bodies of some early polar explorers were preserved un-under ice so well that they looked as if they had died only yesterday. On the other hand, a corpse in a damp tropical climate can be reduced to a skeleton in a matter of weeks. One reason is insects.

Insects, Flesh and Time

Forensic entomologists specialize in two things: insects and dead flesh. What does one have to do with the other? Not long after people die, the flies begin arriving. They come to feed on the flesh and blood. They also lay their eggs. These turn into maggots, which develop into adult flies.

Flies are often first on the scene. A female fly can smell dead flesh up to 2.4 km (1.5 miles) away. They can show up ten minutes after death if the body is out in the open air. They quickly lay thousands of eggs in the body's mouth, nose and eyes. Around twelve hours later, the eggs hatch into maggots. These feed on the flesh.

After twenty-four hours or so, the beetles arrive. Twenty-four hours after that, millipedes and spiders come. They feed on the maggots and beetles. The different bugs hold clues to when the victim died.

Maggots (left) and flies (above) give clues about how long a person has been dead.

Reconstructing the Crime

Two dirt bikers approached a burned-out car on a country road. They didn't know what to expect. In the back seat lay a charred body. It was covered in maggots.

Burning a dead body will not destroy evidence from a crime.

After the police had a look, they called in a team of forensic investigators. The body was taken in for a post-mortem.

The post-mortem showed that maggots were not just on the body's surface. There were also maggots inside the body. These maggots had been burned to death. The post-mortem also revealed knife marks on the victim's spine.

Based on this evidence, the team reconstructed the crime. First, the victim must have been stabbed to death and left in the car. Then the flies arrived and laid eggs. They hatched into maggots. The maggots ate their way into the brain. This process would take about two weeks.

That meant the killers must have returned to the car two weeks after the murder to set it on fire. Maybe they thought the fire would burn up the corpse and hide the evidence. After the fire, flies returned to lay more eggs on the charred flesh.

A Passion for the Job

How do forensic scientists feel about their work? Dr Angela Gallop says, 'The science is relevant to everyday life...This feeling that you are making a contribution to society and using your scientific background gives great satisfaction.'

The Investigation Ends

As we have seen, a lot of work goes into a criminal investigation. Evidence is gathered from the crime scene by police officers, SOCOs and the forensic scientists. If a death has occurred, the body is taken to the morgue. The forensic scientist performs a post-mortem and sends samples of tissues and fluids to labs for testing. If the body has been dead for a long time, a forensic entomologist may examine it. If only bones remain, a forensic anthropologist will look them over.

Once a forensic scientist has examined the corpse, a coroner determines whether the death was natural or not. A coroner is responsible for investigating all violent or unnatural deaths, or sudden deaths of unknown causes. He or she is responsible for officially determining the time and cause of death. If the death was unnatural, an inquest begins – to find out who the deceased was as well as how and when they died.

chapter 5

New Technologies

Forensic science techniques and tools continue to advance. They all help to answer the vital questions: Who is the victim? What is the cause of death? What is the time of death? Who is the criminal?

Scientists keep searching for new and better ways to identify people's unique characteristics. One way uses chromatography. That's the process of breaking down a chemical mixture into its different ingredients.

Human perspiration is a chemical mixture. If we think of sweat as perfume, then we each have our own unique scent. Scientists are trying to use chromatography to make a chemical profile of perspiration. One day, people could be positively identified by the tiny traces of their body odour.

IT'S A FACT!

The maximum amount of sweat a person can produce in an hour is about 3 litres.

Live-Scan Fingerprinting

Even tools that have been around for a while are being improved. Fingerprinting is one example. Live-scan fingerprinting is a new way to take prints.

People place their fingertips on a screen. A video scanner turns the prints into electronic images. This takes about five minutes. Live-scan machines are small and portable. Police can take them along wherever they go. They can feed electronic fingerprint images into computer databases, just like ink and paper images. Police can easily compare the prints with the millions of fingerprints on file.

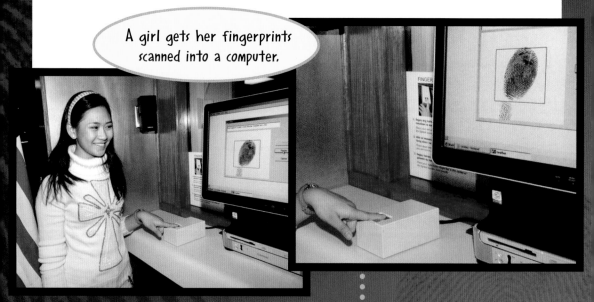

A girl gets her fingerprints scanned into a computer.

Caught by His Skin

Low copy number (LCN) DNA is a new, supersensitive DNA technology. LCN allows scientists to produce a DNA profile from a very, very small sample. The next case shows how sensitive it is.

In 1993 an armed robber stole about £38,000 from a business in Hull, Yorkshire. The only evidence left by the thief was the mask he'd used.

It was a woman's nylon stocking. The police hoped to find traces of blood, sweat or saliva on the nylon. However, they only found – twenty-five skin cells. This was not enough to test the DNA.

At least, that was true at the time. However, technology has improved and in 2004, investigators looked at the evidence again. Using LCN, they could test the skin cells and get a DNA profile.

The profile led police to Andrew Pearson. During Pearson's trial, a forensics expert was called to the witness stand. What were the chances that the skin cells on the stocking could have come from another man and not Andrew Pearson? A billion to one, the expert said. Pearson was found guilty and sentenced to prison.

Computers and Faces

New computer techniques are changing the art of facial reconstruction. Computer programs make the process simpler and faster than the clay method (see page 30). The computer scans the victim's skull from all sides. From these scans, the software creates the skin, hair, ears, eyes, nose and other facial features.

The electronic image can then be easily changed. The nose can be tilted at a different angle. The hair can be re-arranged, the eyes reshaped and so forth. These changes are much faster and easier than changing a clay model. Forensic scientist Wally Schier

A scientist demonstrates how facial recognition software works.

says, 'Instead of being stuck with the model we made today, and having to completely redo it to account for . . . variations, we can do one model, make the adjustments on-screen and print out all the possibilities for investigators'.

And that's not all. Software can 'age' a face, or make it look older. Let's say police want to find someone who went missing ten years earlier. All they have is a photo taken at the age of six.

How would this person look at sixteen? Computer software can 'predict' the changes, based on what we know about ageing. Our ears get longer as we get older, for instance, so the software lengthens the ears. Since the software 'knows' how the other features age, it can do the same thing to the rest of the face. These 'aged' photos are then given out to law enforcement agencies. The photos help police search for the missing person.

This photo shows Cherrie Mahan at age eight. She was kidnapped in 1985.

This image is a computerized age progression that shows what Cherrie Mahan might have looked like at twenty-three.

How Have I Changed?

Find a photograph of you when you were younger. Hold it up next to your face, and look in a mirror. Look closely at your hair, nose, eyes and ears. How have your features changed over the years?

42

DNA Database

As forensic techniques and tools advance, experts keep looking for new ways to bring them together. Computers are the key.

The first DNA database was launched at the Home Office's Forensic Science Laboratory in Birmingham in 1995. Anyone accused or convicted of a criminal offence in the United Kingdom has their DNA taken and recorded on the database as a unique DNA profile. If a suspect is later found to be innocent, his or her DNA profile is removed.

Within months of launching the database the Forensic Science Laboratory got their first match – a suspect in Derbyshire was arrested. His DNA sample matched that of evidence left at the crime scene being investigated. Since then the database has grown to about two million suspect and criminal DNA profiles. Over 10,000 arrests have been made thanks to these important records, including solving over 1,000 murder cases and 1,800 rapes.

As forensic scientist Paul Kirk says 'Wherever [the criminal] steps, whatever he touches, whatever he leaves, even unconsciously, will serve as silent witness against him. . . . This is evidence that does not forget'. Meanwhile, forensic scientists keep working on new and improved ways to get this evidence to reveal its secrets.

Glossary

case study: a detailed description of how investigators solved a crime

chain of custody: the transfer of a piece of evidence from one police officer or investigator to another until it is used in court

coroner: a coroner is responsible for investigating all violent or unnatural deaths, or sudden deaths of unknown causes

crime scene: place where a crime has been committed

Death Row: the place in prison where people sentenced to death in the US are held

deoxyribonucleic acid (DNA): a single molecule in a cell containing the instructions for growing and operating that organism

DNA profile: unique strands of DNA that can identify a person, like fingerprints

facial reconstruction: making a likeness of a person's face using only the skull as reference. This can be done by a forensic artist with clay or a computer technician using special software.

fingerprinting: using ink and paper or computer technology to take impressions of the markings on a person's fingertips

forensic anthropologist: expert who uses skeletal remains to reveal details about how victims died and how they looked when they were alive

forensic entomologist: expert who examines the different types of insect life found on corpses at crime scenes to work out the time of death

forensic science: science used in a court of law

forensic scientist: medical doctor who specializes in examining bodies at crime scenes and doing post-mortems to determine time and cause of death

morgue: place where victims' bodies are kept before they are buried

post-mortem: medical examination of a dead body to find the cause of death

Scene of Crime Officer (SOCO): an officer who investigates a crime scene in search of forensic evidence; known as Crime Scene Investigators (CSIs) in the US of America

trace evidence: bits of evidence found at a crime scene, such as skin cells or carpet fibres

Source Notes

pp 10–11,'Forensic Science Resources—Facts and Figures,' *National Criminal Justice Reference Service*, nd, http://ncjrs.org/forensic/facts.html (22 December 2005).

p 35, Katherine Ramsland, 'All About Autopsies and Dr Michael Baden,' *CrimeLibrary.com*, nd, http://www.crimelibrary.com/criminal_mind/forensics/autopsy/3.html (27 February 2006).

p 37, Katherine Ramsland, 'All About Crime Scene Analysis,' *CrimeLibrary.com*, nd, http://www.crimelibrary.com/criminal_mind/forensics/crimescene/7.html (27 February 2006).

p 37, Laura Jastram, 'Forensic Scientist Uncovers Truth,' *Daily Illini*, February 4 2004, www.illinimedia.com/di/features/367 (5 January 2005).

p 42, N E Genge, *The Forensic Casebook: The Science of Crime Scene Investigation*, (New York: Ballantine Books, 2002), 169–170.

p 43, Richard E Bisbing, 'Fractured Patterns: Microscopical Investigation of Real Physical Evidence,' *ModernMicroscopy.com*, 2004, http://www.modernmicroscopy.com/main.asp?article=11&page=2 (27 February 2006).

Selected Bibliography

Baden, Michael. *Dead Reckoning: The New Science of Catching Killers.* New York: Simon & Schuster, 2001.

Fridell, Ron. *Decoding Life: Unraveling the Mysteries of the Genome.* Minneapolis: Lerner Publications Company, 2005.

Solving Crimes: Pioneers of Forensic Science. New York: Franklin Watts, 2000.

Friedlander, Mark P, and Terry M Phillips. *When Objects Talk: Solving a Crime with Science.* Minneapolis: Lerner Publications Company, 2001.

Genge, N E *The Forensic Casebook: The Science of Crime Scene Investigation.* New York: Ballantine Books, 2002.

Owen, David. *Hidden Evidence.* Buffalo: Firefly Books, 2000.

Ubelaker, Douglas, and Henry Scammell. *Bones: A Forensic Detective's Casebook.* New York: Edward Burlingame Books, 1992.

Wilson, Colin, and Damon Wilson. *Written in Blood: A History of Forensic Detection.* New York: Carroll and Graf Publishers, 2003.

Further Reading and Websites

Conan Doyle, Sir Arthur. *Adventures of Sherlock Holmes* (Penguin Popular Classics) Penguin Classics, 1994.

Cooper, Chris. *Forensic Science* (Eyewitness Books) Dorling Kindersley Publishing, 2008.

Gifford, Clive. *Crimebusters: How Science Fights Crime* University College Press, 2007.

Platt, Richards. *Forensics* (Kingfisher Knowledge) Kingfisher Books Ltd., 2005.

Prokos, Anna. *Guilty by a Hair: Real-Life DNA Matches* (24/7: Science Behind the Scenes: Forensic Science) Franklin Watts, 2007.

Wiese, Jim. *Detective Science: 40 Crime-Solving, Case-Breaking, Crook-Catching Activities for Kids.* New York: John Wiley & Sons, 1996.

The Sherlock Holmes Museum

http://www.sherlock-holmes.co.uk/home.htm

Who Dunnit?

http://www.cyberbee.com/whodunnit/crime.html

GALWAY COUNTY LIBRARIES

Index

Photo Acknowledgements

The images in this book are used with the permission of: © Bettmann/CORBIS, pp 4, 9 (top), 18, 24 (both); © MELMOTH/AFP/Getty Images, p 5; © Todd Strand/Independent Picture Service, pp 6 (left), 14; © SuperStock, Inc./SuperStock, p 6 (right); AP Photo/Justice Department, p7; © Brad Markel/Liaison/Getty Images, p 8 (left); © Reuters/CORBIS, p 8 (right); © Boyer/Roger Viollet/Getty Images, p 9 (bottom); © Hulton Archive/Getty Images, pp 10, 11; © Surrey Police Force p 12; © Ashley Cooper/CORBIS, p 13 (both); © age fotostock/SuperStock, pp 15 (both), 25 (left); © Mauro Fermariello/Photo Researchers, Inc, pp 16, 33 (top); Agricultural Research Service, USDA, p 17; © Chris Fairclough/Discovery Picture Library, p 22, 23; © Biophoto Associates/Photo Researchers, Inc., p 25 (middle); © Richard T Nowitz/Photo Researchers, Inc, p 25 (right); © AP Photo/Joerg Sarbach, p 26; © SIU/Visuals Unlimited, p 28 (top); © PhotoDisc/Getty Images, pp 28 (bottom), 31; © Culver Pictures, Inc./SuperStock, p 29; © Michael Donne, University of Manchester/Photo Researchers, Inc, p 30 (both); © Shephard Sherbell/CORBIS SABA, p 33 (bottom); © Take 2 Productions/Ken Kaminesky/CORBIS, p 34; © R F Ashley/Visuals Unlimited, p 36 (left); © C P Hickman/Visuals Unlimited, p 36 (right); © Gala/SuperStock, p 37; © Jay Directo/AFP/Getty Images, p 40 (both); © Sam Ogden/Photo Researchers, Inc, p 41.

Front Cover: © Todd Strand/Independent Picture Service (top); © Royalty-Free/CORBIS (centre); © PhotoDisc/Getty Images (bottom).

This book was first published in the United States of America in 2007.
Text copyright © 2007 by Ron Fridell

GALWAY COUNTY LIBRARIES

About the Author

Ron Fridell has written for radio, television and newspapers. He has also written books about the Human Genome Project and the use of DNA to solve crimes. In addition to writing books, Fridell regularly visits libraries and schools to conduct workshops on non-fiction writing.